T0128856

The Do Not Rent List

Todd Ruffin Sr.

It's A Customer Warning Not Customer Service
Because
The Customer is **NOT** always Right!

THE DO NOT RENT LIST

iUniverse books may be ordered through booksellers or by contacting:

iUniverse
1663 Liberty Drive
Bloomington, IN 47403
www.iuniverse.com
1-800-Authors (1-800-288-4677)

ISBN: 978-1-4917-6937-9 (sc)
ISBN: 978-1-4917-6938-6 (e)

Print information available on the last page.

iUniverse rev. date: 07/07/2015

On a Need-to-Know Basis— and You Definitely Need to Know

In my twenty-plus years of working in the customer-service industry, I've learned many things. One is not necessarily more important than the other; however, the combined information is valuable. I've managed people and supervised stores, but I spent almost thirteen years of my career putting people on what we in the industry call the "Do Not Rent" list. It's a database of customers whom the company wishes to never see again. These customers have committed atrocious acts, everything from violence, shoplifting, and petty crimes to felony assault and even murder. Dealing with these people opened my eyes to an underground world of human disappointment and indignity: people renting cars and furniture in order to steal them from you or use the car to commit a crime. You never know if you can trust the would-be renter standing in front of you. That type of person makes you not want to go to work every day, but that's why the Do Not Rent list exists. To even the odds!

If you're not on the list, keep being a good renter and a good customer. But if you are on the list, I wonder if one of the true stories in this book is yours. Are you on the DNR list? The names have been changed in the book to protect the privacy of the not-so-innocent. I don't know why I bothered to do that, because most of them are quite despicable. What it really boils down to is that the things these people do in rental cars (other than stealing them) typically cause some type of damage to the vehicle, and when that happens, the renter/customer is ultimately responsible to pay for any and all damages to the vehicle, regardless of how the damages occurred. That's what you agree to when you sign a rental contract. When you rent that car—meaning you are signing a *binding, legal* contract—make sure you are completely covered for anything and everything that may happen to that car during your rental period. This is how you do it.

There are three ways to cover yourself: (1) through your own personal lines insurance policy, which will not transfer to the rental car if you're renting for business; (2) through your credit-card coverage program, but you should read the fine print of the terms and conditions of coverage; or (3) by purchasing the collision damage waiver from the rental-car agency.

Now I know what you're saying. "That damage waiver crap is a scam." But is it really? I mean, let's be honest. Who wins in that deal? Say you rent a car for the weekend and it costs you $145, including the damage waiver, which costs $18 a day, or $54. Then the vehicle gets a cracked windshield, hit while parked, sideswiped on the highway, or rear-ended at a red light—or a safe drops out of a ten-story building on top of the car and totals it. You are covered as long as you don't violate the terms and conditions of the rental agreement, which could void the damage waiver. For any damage between $55 and $50,000 (or the total value of the car), you have won! So, honestly, how is that a scam? I mean, you've paid thousands of dollars to your own insurance company through the years with no payoff. Think about it. How can it be a scam by the rental-car company? The rental company loses big-time when a car is damaged and covered by the damage waiver because it costs them way more money to repair the car as oppose to how much money they collected from you buying the collision damage waiver. Truth be told—it's not a scam; it's all sales and revenue which equals capitalism just like anything else in the United States, but the benefit of a collision damage waiver is clearly yours (the renter).

The Do Not Rent List

It's a customer WARNING not customer service

because

The customer is NOT always right!

Introduction

The purpose of this book is to shed light on one of the more familiar sayings known to man: "The customer is always right." It's well known in the service industry, but I have no qualms about disagreeing with that statement because I have seen the light, which I will now shed upon you!

The customer is *not* always right, and that is a fact. As you turn each page in this book, you will become more and more convinced of that. The phrase is thought to have been coined by several extremely successful businessmen in the late 1800s. These men were the greatest entrepreneurs of their time, and in creating this phrase (which became a worldwide phenomenon), they intended to soothe consumers and build a trust between their retail operations and their strong customer bases. In German the phrase is *der Kunde ist König* and loosely translates into "The customer is king." Their intention was not to have customers think they were kings and queens, but by the year 1914, it was evident in retail locations across the globe that customers did believe that wholeheartedly. Customers seemed to develop ulterior motives when it came to being "always right," and it just got worse as the years went by until we were left with the things crazy customers like to do today, commit crimes anywhere and everywhere they can!

One thing is for sure, though: this ends now! As you read this book, you will begin to see that customers can be coldhearted, manipulative, self-serving people who honestly don't deserve the good customer service that is typically provided every day. The eerie thing is that no one has any idea how evil a customer is until after his/her evil act is committed. Realistically, it would take a crystal ball to see beforehand how bad these customers are. That's why The Do Not Rent list is so important. A customer gets one chance to commit these acts and show his or her true colors, after which this person is marked forever and cannot hurt another person or property in their wicked ways or with the use of a rental car.

The stories you will read involve death, damage, armed robbery, shootings, high-speed chases, and just plain lunatic behavior by people who seemed to be average. As it turns out, they should have been on the DNR list a long time ago. Maybe, then, some of the victims would never have been hurt, and some of the accidents and damages may have never occurred. Maybe even a life could have been saved.

You are about to read some of the most deplorable true stories you could ever come across. It's important to know that all of these stories are 100 percent real. The names have been changed for privacy, but none of the renters you are going to read about deserve your pity, admiration, or sorrow. The victims do, but not the renters. The sad truth about all of these stories is that someone or some business got hurt physically or financially. That being said, you will quickly realize that the renter did not care one bit. From the lighthearted stories that only involve the car being damaged to the more serious ones involving felonies committed through the use of the vehicle, the renters do not care. It's a shame that people can actually be this evil, but, hey, that's why these people are on the Do Not Rent list.

Chapter 1

Renters with Victims

Hit-and-Run Death Resulting

In this especially heinous story, a life was taken through the use of a rental car which is why I'm opening the book with it. Even though it may not have been done purposefully, that does not change the fact that a man is dead. It goes without saying that some renters were worse than others. To be honest, it would be difficult to pick which one was the worst. But I guess the long and short of it is that you can make that choice for yourself. I do have to tell you though that this first woman is quite despicable. You be the judge.

One Monday morning in 2008, I received a call from the police department regarding the previous rainy Saturday night. The police wanted to verify the name of the person who rented a 2008 Dodge Avenger. Initially I told the officer that we could not provide that information without an administrative subpoena. As quickly as I told him that, the officer advised me of a most heinous crime: a pedestrian hit and run with one of our cars, "death resulting." All I needed to hear were the words pedestrian hit and run, but when he said "death resulting," I was floored. Completely shocked. It appeared that our renter had killed a pedestrian.

I immediately gave the officer all the information he needed, and he told me someone would fax over the administrative subpoena. He thanked me for my help, and that was the end of the call; however, it was not the end of this tragedy. I immediately reported this to my bosses, and soon enough everyone on the job knew about it, including the branch that rented the woman the car. Immediately that branch started looking for the renter and the car, but they could not find either one.

The police found the car fairly fast. It was abandoned in a vacant lot near the scene of the accident. A smashed windshield stained with blood from the impact was evident, along with hood and grill damage. The police department told us that a lot of stolen cars got dumped there. Now that they had her information, a warrant went out for her arrest, and a manhunt began. But just as quickly as they started the hunt, it ended. She turned herself in that afternoon, reportedly telling the police that she didn't know she had hit someone. I guess she didn't know she had dumped the car either!

 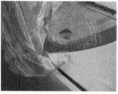 

Everyone wanted her behind bars because of the particular carelessness she'd shown, for if she had stopped after hitting the pedestrian and called 911, it's possible that the victim could have survived. If he had survived, she would not be in jail—and maybe she would not be on the DNR list permanently!

This particular story points directly to why the DNR list is necessary. It shows you how careless people are. It directly flies in the face of "the customer is always right" concept and proves that the customer is dead wrong, pardon the pun. The rest of the stories you will read in this book will confirm my theory that the DNR list is a welcomed customer-warning signal that all businesses wish they could have. If the renter of this next vehicle had been on the list, the driver would never have been behind the wheel. It's weird how a small detail like that can play out, change an entire string of circumstances, and in turn change many people's lives.

<u>Shots Fired</u>

The next renter was wrong in more ways than one because he gave the rental car to a friend, not knowing how crazy that friend was. In what can only be described as temporary insanity, this driver attempted to kill a police officer. Just as in the previous story, a life was at risk, but the tables quickly turned, and justice prevailed.

"To protect and serve" is the motto of most police agencies around the country. On a daily basis, officers and detectives put their lives on the line to look out for us. But what happens when the officers need protecting?

Back in the fall of 2008, around eleven o'clock one night, this particular officer was on the job, conducting what he thought was a routine traffic stop on a rental vehicle. He handled the situation just as he did any vehicle he stopped: the officer was unassuming and nonjudgmental toward the driver, expecting him to stop as directed and follow his commands. On this Wednesday night though, he would get more than he bargained for because the driver of the vehicle had something else in mind.

After stopping the vehicle and running the plates on the computer, the officer got out of his car and approached the rental car. That's when things went haywire. As the officer neared the vehicle, the driver slipped the car into gear, stomped on the gas pedal and veered toward the officer. The officer was completely caught by surprise and tried to protect himself, but it was too late. Boom! He was hit. Falling to the ground, the officer still had enough quick wit to draw his weapon. In doing so he got up and was able to fire two rounds into the windshield of the car, possibly hitting the driver. Hobbling on one leg and standing in the middle of the street, he watched as the car sped off erratically. He then called in to dispatch, "Shots fired, officer down." Automatically the call went out on this rental vehicle, and every cop within visual distance of a red car was looking for this guy, including the state police. It didn't take long for the police to find the car and the occupants, mainly because the driver had been hit by one of the officer's bullets and was hurt. He could not go too far and ended up stopping just a few miles from the site of the incident.

The officer and the suspects—the driver and his passenger—were taken to the hospital for their injuries and then released after several hours. Consequently, the suspects were arrested and charged with assaulting a police officer and numerous other charges.

Neither suspect turned out to be the renter of the vehicle, but the renter didn't report the vehicle stolen either. So this turned out to be an unauthorized driver situation in regard to the rental vehicle. What sucks for the renter in a situation like this is that no matter what damage occurs or how it occurs, the renter is responsible to pay for those damages based on the contract. The fact that the officer fired two rounds through the windshield and into the upholstery would make you think that the police department's insurance would pay for it, but no, it doesn't work that way. The police have what is called "municipal immunity" in a situation like this. They are not responsible; the renter is—for the windshield, the bloodstains, the upholstery, everything. The unauthorized driver automatically puts the renter on the DNR list. In this situation, the renter had no intention of paying for the damages, which were well over $2,000. So the renter, although he was not in the car, made it onto the DNR list with no hope of ever renting again.

Those two cases are similar only in that they contain people breaking the law while using a rental car and making the DNR list forever. If you haven't heard of the Do Not Rent list, perhaps that is a blessing. Clearly it could mean you've never been put on the list, but do you know of someone who has? This next criminal specifically rented a car to commit his crimes, and he got away with it for a while too. He was a perfect candidate for the Do Not Rent list.

Todd Ruffin Sr.

<u>Renting for Criminal Purposes</u>

We received a call from the local police department. The detective on the phone gave me the license plate number, make, and model of one of our vehicles and said he needed to know who had rented the vehicle on three separate dates, all within a three-week period. Why? Because a man wearing a mask had used this vehicle to commit three armed robberies—two at gas stations (one local and the other in the adjoining city) and the third at a bakery, which turned out to be near our renter's home address. After I gave him the information, the detective told me he was coming to the office with a warrant for the rental agreement and a special request for me that had to be done in person. After that call, my coworker Kim and I discussed the situation and got really nervous, wondering what the police would need from us other than the rental agreement.

When the detective arrived, he was up front. "Sir, we're gonna need your assistance to get this guy today," he said. I didn't quite understand what he meant, but I replied, "Sure, whatever you need, we always cooperate with the police." I thought he probably just wanted me to call the guy or something, but oh no, that was not what he wanted. I was about to have the experience of a lifetime! As the detective explained it to me, my knees got rubbery, my stomach felt hollow, and I thought I was going to pass out. He needed me, little ole me in my suit and tie, to help him run a sting operation on this guy to lure him out of his house and into the street so he could arrest him for the armed robberies. Wow! I was floored, and Kim was in complete shock.

I wasn't sure if this was against company policy or if I should just be a good citizen or what, but as we stood there with the detective thinking how we rented a car to a criminal, basically helping him commit these armed robberies, I thought it was the least I could do, and Kim agreed. So off we went to the "staging area."

The staging area was about a mile or so away from the targeted house where the officers prepared and geared up for the intended operation. Kim was my moral support, so she rode with me in case something went wrong. While we were there, the detectives prepped me on the plan and what my duties would be. They needed me to call the renter and tell him I was on the way to his house to switch out his car because of a serious maintenance issue that could not wait. Once I arrived at the house, I needed to get him to come all the way outside, as close to the replacement car as possible (away from the house), so the fifteen officers posted around the perimeter of the house could take him down and enter the house to ward off any possible accomplices who might be there. Sounds easy right? Well, I can tell you, without a doubt, that while my legs were trembling and my hands were shaking, whether or not this was easy did not cross my mind. What did cross my mind was if something were to go horribly wrong, was I ready to die today or not?

At the staging area, everyone prepped—plainclothes officers, uniformed officers, and SWAT team officers. Everyone put on their bulletproof vests, filled their gun clips with live bullets, and put on their war paint. The detective put a protective bulletproof vest on me (under my winter coat), which really made me see how serious this thing was. Once everyone was set, we jumped into the vehicles and I made the call to the renter, advising him that I would be at his house in ten minutes. As I made that call, all the tactical officers were getting into position, and once I finished, the detective and I drove to one block away from the renter's house. Then we waited ten minutes. That was the longest ten minutes of my life.

I pulled the rental car up to the curb and parked directly in front of the renter's house. I could see our rental car sitting in his driveway all the way up to the front of his garage. The detective accompanied me as we exited the car and headed to the side door of the house. As I walked up the driveway, I could see the SWAT officer on top of the garage with his rifle, getting his sight set on the target (the side door). I could also see two officers behind the tall shrubs on the right side of the driveway behind the rental car. This was all reassuring, but then the moment of truth arrived. As I reached the door and prepared to ring the doorbell to speak to the armed felon, I was filled with doubt, fear, courage, and anger all at the same time. I was doubtful because I wasn't sure I should be doing this and fearful for both my safety and how this might affect my job. However, courage superseded my fear when I realized that there were a dozen trained officers surrounding this door, and every single one of them would protect me and was ready to shoot to kill this criminal in a split second. So I rang the bell and waited for an answer. The renter's wife opened the door, holding a baby. "Hello, ma'am, I'm here with the replacement rental car for your husband. May I speak to him please?" I said.

"Oh, I can take the keys," she said, which totally blew the whole plan. So thinking quickly, I replied, "Oh, no, ma'am, your husband has to inspect the new vehicle with me and re-sign the contract." She said, "Okay, wait here, and I'll go get him."

The detective and I looked at each other, wondering if this was on the up-and-up. Was she really going to get him, or was our cover blown? At least that's what I was thinking, because at this point I was scared to death. It turned out to be okay, as the renter came to door. "Hello," he said. "Hello, sir, how are you today?" I responded. "Good until you called me for this," he said. "Why do you need the car I'm driving?" Automatically I thought he was on to us, and my fear returned because the renter would not come out of the house. Just then the detective jumped in and said, "There's a recall on the taillights that we need to get done; sorry for the inconvenience." The renter replied "Oh, okay," which gave me instant relief. Thank you, Detective. It looked like we were in the clear, as the renter started to come out of the house, but then he said, "Oh, wait one minute," and walked back inside. The detective reached into his trench coat for his weapon. But then the renter came back and said, "You'll need the key for this car, right?" With a scared-stiff laugh, I responded, "Yes sir, I will."

As the renter slowly walked out of the house, I engaged him in conversation to train his attention on me. We proceeded down the driveway as the detective positioned himself slightly behind the renter to his right. Just then everything became a gigantic countdown. It was intense:

five, four, three, two, one—boom! The detective grabbed the renter's right arm and twisted it behind him. The two officers came rushing out from behind the shrubs, subduing the renter on his left side, and the next thing I knew, the renter was face down in the grass, screaming, "What's going on? What is this? I didn't do it." He yelled out any and everything you could imagine to try to get the officers who were holding him down to take their knees out of his back. When I tell you he was subdued, I mean he was *subdued*! He could not move a muscle. After a few minutes, he quieted down, and four officers picked him up off the ground like a corpse. Each officer was holding one of his limbs.

During this whole event, the renter's wife had made her way outside, holding the baby and throwing a fit. She yelled and screamed that the police had the wrong man and her husband didn't do it. The funny thing was, she didn't even know what the charges were! Some of the officers warded her off, while others searched the house. Meanwhile I just stood there shivering in amazement because I made it through unblemished and unharmed. Now I had to figure out how to drive two rental cars back to the office. As for the renter, he and his wife never had to worry about renting a car again—partly because he went in jail and mainly because his entire household was now on the *permanent* DNR list. They deserved more than that for punishment, but all we could do was ban them both from renting.

This is a perfect example of how crazy people are and the things they do with rental cars. Truthfully, he could have gotten away with it if the police hadn't caught him, and we would have never been the wiser. Armed robbery is a bit more outlandish than our next story although this offender's decision-making skills were seriously suspect.

Stolen Identity

A supposed body shop manager—let's call him Jason—loved to secure rental cars for his customers. In doing so one time, he had the car and the contract delivered to his shop, but the would-be renter—let's call him Louis—was not there. Since this was about business, however, and Jason was a good talker, the company employee left the rental car and contract there, with Jason's promise that he would drop off the signed contract in a few hours. Two hours later he did bring the contract to the rental branch and said the renter was happy with the vehicle.

A week later the police called the home office about this very car. It seemed this vehicle had been involved in two hit-and-run accidents, and the driver of the vehicle was suspicious. Three days earlier he'd hit a small child as he backed out into the street, knocking the child down (luckily not seriously hurting him). Then, on this same day, the driver sideswiped a parked car, smashing the right mirror of the rental car and blowing the rear tire. He kept driving, trying to escape, until the rim collapsed and the car was immobilized. The police officer on the scene said the driver's name was Louis, but the picture on the license was not the person he was looking at so they towed the car, arrested him, and took him to county lockup.

Hours later the rental branch received a call from Jason, the body shop manager. The rental branch manager asked him, "Who is this Louis guy you had us rent a car to? Our car's been towed, he was in a hit-and-run accident, and the police called us. What is going on?" Jason replied, "I'm sorry, man. I didn't mean for any of this to happen, but can you tell the police you're not pressing charges on your damaged car so I can get out of jail?" It turns out that Jason was the perpetrator, and he used his one phone call to call us, trying to avoid prosecution. Sorry, Jason, but you hit a child and fled the scene. It was out of our hands and in the control of the district attorney. But even if we did have a say, we would have said to charge him, because this guy was going to be on the Do Not Rent list for life. He owed us money for damages to the car that we would never see, and he committed several crimes. The only thing to be learned from that guy is how to be guilty.

The Killer Rental

There are some things that are worse than others, and this is one of them. It's a sad story that must be told. As stated earlier, no one knew fifty years ago that the DNR list would need to be in place to prevent murderers from renting cars in order to commit their crimes. But, lo and behold, in today's world it is necessary! The long and short of the business is that we never truly know what a renter is going to do with a rental car. Renters do not make their intentions known, and there's no way to find out what they are doing with the cars until the deed is done—particularly when they commit heinous crimes like this one did.

In the late 1990s, a string of murders took place in a small New England town. By the time the crimes were solved and the killer was caught, the body count was up to five. All of the victims were prostitutes. They were kidnapped, raped, killed, and dismembered by one of our renters. Reportedly after strangling the women to death he would dismember them with a saw, put the body parts in garbage bags, and scatter the bags in several dumpsters around the neighborhood. He would only use the rental vehicle for a few hours to pick up the women and kill them then use the car to disburse their body parts around town in different dumpsters. Returning the car quickly aided in his attempts to avoid detection by not being seen with the car again as the hooker's last customer. When he was caught, he told the police he learned how to do this by watching TV.

This was the most gruesome crime that small town had ever seen, and it will go down in history as such. After two years, the police finally got a viable lead (a phone call on the police tip line) and brought a suspect in for questioning. Initially he denied everything. But after six hours of interrogation, he gave in. He confessed to everything and led police to all the evidence. In the end, the killer was quoted as saying, "I'm sorry. I don't know why I did it. It was an urge I couldn't control, and I'm glad you caught me because I wasn't going to be able to stop."

I checked on his case when I was writing this book, and he is serving a life sentence with no chance of parole. So without a doubt he will never rent a car again.

That story was a true tragedy. What do you do when tragedy occurs in your family? Hopefully you bond together more than ever and become stronger. In this next story, the renter was faced with that very question. Tragedy struck, and the rental branch had the unfortunate job of calling the renter to inform her that her son had been murdered in the rental car. That has to be the worst phone call any employee has ever had to make.

Bad News That Got Worse

Technically, any rental car that comes back with damage (including bullet holes and blood spatter throughout the interior) that occurred during the use of the car by an unauthorized driver voids the contract and violates the rental agreement. So even if the renter purchased the collision damage waiver, he or she remains responsible and must pay for the damage. That is exactly what happened here, and it was a case of going from bad to worse. It involved an unauthorized driver who happened to be the renter's son. And it did involve some damage for which, tragically, the renter remained responsible.

It was the summer of 2006, and the car was a black Chevy Malibu. There was nothing special about the car, just tan cloth seats with a regular-style interior, no sunroof or anything. The only thing special about this car was the terrible incident destined to occur inside it. The renter was a female in her forties, and unbeknownst to her on this warm summer night, her seventeen-year-old son decided to take the rental car for a little joyride with a friend. They ended up in a city about thirty miles from home in a bad neighborhood, one well known for drug activity. They parked in an apartment building's parking lot where someone got into the car with them. The three youths were seen sitting in the car together. One thing led to another and "pop-pop." Shots rang out from inside the car. The kid's friend took off running, and so did the shooter, but the renter's son did not. He was the one hit by the bullets, and he lay there unconscious, bleeding to death while waiting for help to arrive. Within minutes the police were there, and within hours our airport rental location got a call from the police that a seventeen-year-old boy had just been killed in our car and no one was around to witness the crime.

The next morning, the airport branch called the local branch where the car had been rented, and within an hour it seemed as if the whole company knew what happened: another fatality in one of the rental cars. And someone had to call the renter to speak with her about this. We assumed that the police had already reached her, but the sad thing was that this woman had just lost her son and now one of us had to have a conversation with her about the damage (bullet holes and blood spatter) in the car.

You would think that we'd be mentally equipped for something like this, but believe me when I tell you, there is no preparing for this kind of tragedy. How do you ask a woman whose son was just murdered to pay for the damage caused by the killer? How do you explain to her that although she lost her son, she was now banned from renting with us because he was an unauthorized driver? I don't necessarily know the answers to these questions, but I do know one thing for sure: you do not do it with a smile!

Chapter 2

Rentals That Never Should've Occurred—*Ever*!

Family Hurts

We all believe that we are able to trust family without question. Where is that written? That's what I would like to know. Some would argue that the truth is family will use you, harm you, and burn you quicker than any stranger you meet. That is why this story is particularly cruel. This renter's family member had no regard for trust, truth, or doing the right thing on any level. Family can hurt you so bad that it leaves you speechless and on the Do Not Rent list.

A woman rented a vehicle for work purposes. Well, at least that's what she told us. But when an accident occurred, it was her niece who was driving the rental car, supposedly without her permission. This was a perfectly new car ruined with only 225 miles on it—a candy-apple-red Nissan Altima with a sunroof, tilt wheel, and leather seats. The niece in vehicle one was traveling north behind vehicle two on a roadway with one lane in each direction. As they approached the intersection, vehicle two slowed down and put his directional signal on to turn left. Vehicle one then attempted to pass vehicle two on the left by crossing over the double yellow lines and struck the fender and front bumper of vehicle two's driver's side. This accident was no doubt the fault of the renter's niece, an unauthorized driver.

Six months later, Mrs. Renter wanted to rent another car from us, but we told her no; she was on the Do Not Rent list because of the unauthorized driver incident. Her story was that she was at work while the car was at home and again that her niece took the car without her permission. Now correct me if I'm wrong, but if you rented the car "for work" and you're at work, shouldn't the car be at work with you? Sorry, lady, *no* car for you. You don't have to go home, but you have to get the hell outta here! You're on the DNR list.

There are acts of pure stupidity, silly acts, and actions that are downright insane. This next story will allow you to choose which one you think best applies to it. Getting tattoos is one thing, but this is on a whole other level.

The Senator of Stupid

In one of the most idiotic moves you will read about in this book, the Senator of Stupid takes first prize as Idiot of the Year. This guy cost us about ninety days' loss of use on a vehicle because of his terrific personality! In his case, a mind is a terrible thing to waste, so he wasted it.

In 2008 we rented this young man a brand-new, all-leather, fully loaded Volkswagen Jetta with only thirty-five miles on it. He'd been in the rental a little less than a week when, on this particular day, he was about to have the worst accident you could ever have without the car moving.

Our Boy Scout set the accident in motion by doing something that I would strongly advise against. At approximately one thirty in the afternoon, according to the police report, the renter sat in the driver's seat of the brand-new Jetta in his driveway with a loaded handgun. As he sat in the vehicle toying with the weapon, you guessed it, the gun fired. He accidentally shot himself! Yes, the bullet went clean through his leg. It also went through the edge of the seat and into the plastic inner part of the door panel, stopping once it hit the metal part of the inner driver's side door. It left a dent that you could clearly see protruding from the outside of the door, and the bullet just dangled inside.

Well, the problem was that since this was a brand-new vehicle from the first production date, there were no spare seats and door panel parts produced yet. So we had to wait for them to be made. We couldn't rent it without a door panel and seat, and we couldn't use the original parts, because, even after attempting to clean it, once there's blood contamination inside the seat cushion and anywhere else the bullet traveled, let's just say it's not safe. Can you say "biohazard"? Legally speaking, according to the rental agreement, the renter is always responsible for any and all damage unless he or she purchased the damage waiver, which this young man did not. Try telling him that. That guy should be on the DNR list for life. Why? For being stupid! Who the hell shoots himself in the leg in a rental car? I wouldn't trust this guy with a bag of oranges, much less another rental.

Trust is a combination of love, honesty, and learned behavior. Bestowing trust upon someone should be from a place in your relationship where your mutual respect for one another lies heavy, deep, and solid as a rock. You don't just pull trust off the bottom of your shoe like dirty, rotten gum you just stepped in.

In this next story, it would appear that the renter chose the dirty, rotten gum approach to her circle of trust. Her trust level seemed to be the equivalent of pissing into the wind. Whomever it landed on, that's whom she would trust.

A Young Girl Thirteen Years Later

Back in 1996, a young girl rented a car from us. As soon as she got home, her cousin told her he needed to go to the store. So instead of being suspicious or even erring on the side of caution, she said, "Sure, you can use my rental car to go to the store." She never asked what store, how long he would be gone, or why he needed to go so badly.

Two hours later the vehicle was involved in a high-speed police chase three towns over. Guns were drawn, and the car crashed. The perpetrator and so-called cousin was face down in the dirt with a cop's knee in his back. I guess what he meant to say was that he needed to go "knock over a store at gunpoint," because that's what he did.

Approximately thirteen years later, in 2009, the young girl was now thirtysomething and had kids, a house, cars, and a husband. Unfortunately she also had an insurance claim for comprehensive damage to her car and needed a rental car. Her insurance company would repair it and pay for her rental, but when she packed up the kids, dropped off the car at the shop, and waited with the kids to get the rental car, this is what happened. They typed her name into the computer and, you guessed it, she popped up on the DNR list. The employee had to tell her, "I'm sorry, Miss, but we cannot rent you a car. It seems there was an incident back in 1996 with the last rental car you had with us. Yes, there's a huge balance, thousands of dollars owed for damages. Here's the phone number you can call to speak with someone about getting off the DNR list." Do you think she legitimately forgot? How can anyone forget something like that?

The next story could never be forgotten because it affected two lives: the renter and his brother. It's a story of simple, even laughable frustration. There are no complicated laws or ridiculous claims of innocence. It's just a stupid mistake that will come back to bite the renter in the ass for many years to come. It will do the same for his brother too.

All in the Family

It's said that one bad decision can last a lifetime. But in this case one bad decision will last for two lifetimes. Two years after the fact, it's a good news/bad news situation for this banned renter. David (the renter) came from the pride of America's armed forces, the United States Army. This soldier, while home on leave, rented a car to get around so he wouldn't have to burden his family to take him here and there. But on the day he was to ship out, he told his brother to go ahead and take the rental car to the store to get a few things and then come back to pick him up. How many times have we heard that scenario? So David's brother, let's call him Adam, did just that. He went to the store, but on the way back he added a little something extra to the trip: an accident!

At kind of a weird intersection, Adam was in the left-turn lane waiting for the green light to turn onto a one-way road with two distinct lanes of travel. The other car was directly across from him, turning right onto the same one-way road. Now, when you turn left onto a one-way roadway with two travel lanes, you are supposed to turn into the left lane and stay there, or if you are turning right onto that roadway, the same rule applies: stay to the right. Poor Adam did the right thing and turned left on green into the left lane, but the other car didn't. She made a gigantic, wide right turn into his lane, and *boom*, they crashed. The woman blamed Adam because physically his car hit her car, but Adam said, "You cut right in front of my lane of travel. What the hell were you doing?" When the police arrived, what did they say? The winner is: Mrs. Right Turn. You are at fault for this accident, and here's your prize—a shiny golden ticket payable by cash or credit card at your local police department.

We had an unauthorized driver, an accident with a third party at fault, and an out-of-state renter. So once we got our car back and collected his deductible ($500), he left town and a battle began—a battle between us and the other driver's insurance company. The insurance company claimed Adam was at fault because he struck her vehicle and that there was a supplement to the police report because the insured complained about the ticket so much that the officer rescinded the citation. Wait, wait, wait. Did you say rescinded the ticket? Oh my God, is she a nun or something? Can you believe this? When have you ever been able to have a traffic citation rescinded because you disagreed with it? Never, right? Only God knows how she was able to get away with that, but one thing was for sure: this was the beginning of the end for our renter and his brother.

The damages were fairly extensive on this claim. It wasn't just a regular dented bumper that could be repaired and painted. Sometimes when accidents occur, damage travels through the panels of the affected areas of the car. What I mean is the front bumper may be the direct point of impact, but the force of the collision can be so strong that the edges of the bumper push back into the adjacent panel, such as the fender, hood, or quarter. When that happens, it causes the panels to buckle and push each other up or down. It's all relative, but the important thing to remember is that most often the damage on a car will not just be the damage you see. There is almost always underlying damage, which was the case for David and Adam to the tune of almost $3,000. And since the at-fault party was fighting it, saying the accident was Adam's fault, both of them were on the hook for all the damages.

But here's the kicker. David was redeployed in the Army and was unreachable in a foreign country. Adam (the unauthorized driver) was still here clueless, jobless, and penniless, so the $3,000 was not coming from him anytime soon. All that was left to do was to put these two on the Do Not Rent list and send them to collections. When you owe the rental-car company thousands of dollars, you definitely make it onto the list. So don't try to rent from that company later in life. Your debt will still be waiting for you forever and ever—amen.

Keep Your Affairs in Order

Unlike the last renter, this one may have learned from her mistakes. When you go to visit your family and/or people back home, always make sure you have your affairs in order. You never know how a small deal (I thought it was nothing) can come back to haunt you.

In 2009 a young woman rented a car with us. She hadn't been home in a few years and was quite excited about flying almost two thousand miles to the East Coast to see her family and friends. She would be visiting them for about six to eight weeks so figured she'd rent a car while she was there. She rented a brand-new Nissan Altima and was the first person to drive it, and everything went smoothly at first.

Then, about a month into the rental, she got into a small fender bender. Not bad, right? Well, it got worse because when the police arrived, they almost arrested her. She was cited for driving on a suspended license, a license she didn't even have anymore. Her license from this state had been suspended in 2005, meaning her right to drive in our state was revoked! The police could have taken her straight to jail, but she claimed she never knew it had been suspended and since then had gotten a new license where she lived now. They didn't lock her up, but here's the awful part. Although the car was *drivable* after the fender bender, the police had it towed. The damage was minor, but, oh my God, the tow bill hurt! That damn bill was more than $500! And guess who was on the hook to pay it. She's now on the Do Not Rent list until further notice or until she does pay it! That sweet girl from next door won't be renting our cars anymore—just like our next prize-winning renter. He will not be obliged to rent again, but there are plenty of other companies whose cars he can crash.

Damage Is Damage

Throughout the years, we've had the occasional renter complain about the cost of the repairs he or she was responsible for. No big deal—it comes with the territory. This guy, however, took it to a new level. Not only did he disagree with the repairs, which had all kinds of discounts extended, but he also swore on the Bible that he owned a body shop. This is why he proclaimed himself an expert and that his experience in car repair was proof enough for him to see that our repair estimates were inflated.

Now, this guy—let's call him Nick—failed to mention how and why the rental car became damaged. The fact of the matter was that he rented a not-so-stylish Kia Rio, but I guess he had something valuable in it that someone wanted or someone wanted to steal the car from him for general purposes. Maybe someone just didn't like him (which I could understand). Clearly someone had taken a crowbar to both front doors, attempting to pry them open all along the door frames. The damage was irrefutable. The cost of the repairs was $1,460, of which Nick's insurance company paid $960. This clearly indicated not only that the company agreed with us and thought the repairs were fair but also that the damage was completely the responsibility of the insured. After all, he did sign a rental agreement in which he agreed to be responsible for any and all damage that might happen to the car.

Months and months went by; letters were sent, and Nick refused to pay his $500 deductible. In several phone calls to him, he angrily called me every name in the book. But I just told him, "Calling me names won't make this go away, and believe me when I say you'll regret it if you don't pay." He never paid, and the file went to the collection agency, at which point good ole Nick was no longer obliged to rent with us. Being the fool that he was, he played games with the collection company too, telling the company representative he would pay it the next week or that the check was in the mail. He would give the person any crappy excuse he could think of to blow off the company.

Even the file at collections went unpaid until that fateful day one year and four months later when Mr. Nick was out of town, attempting to rent from us at an airport, and he popped up on the Do Not Rent list. Acting shocked, as though he had no idea why he was on DNR, Nick had the rental branch call us. I explained in detail that Mr. Nick didn't pay his deductible for damages. And that's where Nick's story ends, stuck on the Do Not Rent list. Sorry, Nick, no car for you. Better luck next time, buddy boy. I told you that you would regret it—just like the next genius who didn't get what he wanted either.

To Rent or Not to Rent

Renting cars was tough, but renting furniture and appliances was downright crazy. Some of the people I had to deal with were unbelievable. At least when you rented someone a car, that person respected you and knew the company, not the customer, owned the car. When you rent people furniture, they assume it's theirs from day one, delivery day.

When it came to renting merchandise, such as couches, bedroom sets, and TVs, the job was easier said than done. Believe it or not, my worst enemies during those days were the months of November through March (no daylight saving time). It was hard enough delivering furniture and appliances to strange places, but doing it in the dark when it's only five in the evening—well, that's a whole different beast. That's why this story is a keeper. If it wasn't for the darkness outside that day, I may have rented the merchandise anyway, which would have undoubtedly turned into a huge loss for the company and more than likely the loss of my job.

I don't remember the would-be renter's name, and I won't even give this one a pseudonym. There's a reason for that, but first let's do a little background on the chain of events. The order that this person placed at the store was a good one, one that you'd think would be a great moneymaker: a full living-room set and a full dining-room set with table and chairs. An order like that totaled well over a hundred dollars a week back in the 1990s. So it seemed that this business transaction was going to be a good one. Delivery to the address would be easy—or I expected it to be, until I opened the door and walked into the house. The thing about renting furniture is that once the merchandise is delivered to that person/address, it becomes your account. After all, that is your job title: account manager.

This particular delivery, however, was extremely suspect from the start. As soon as I rang the doorbell, the door opened, and a man dressed like a woman was standing in front of me. No biggie—I looked past that and politely asked for the renter. But when the man, wearing a halter top and miniskirt, replied in his deep voice, "Yes, that's me," I saw we had a problem. Because as I looked beyond him into the apartment, I noticed it was completely empty. So I stepped in and said, "Where would you like the stuff to go?" Yet, as I looked around, something told me this was a straight no-go! The walls were bare. The kitchen was empty. The bedrooms, dining room, and living room were empty too. This was feeling like a setup to me. There are people out there who will rent furniture and stuff, have it delivered to a fake address, move it out the next day (stealing it), and it's gone forever. We would never find it. That was exactly what this felt like.

So as I walked around the apartment, I asked again what was ordered. Then I decided to play a little game of my own. "Oh my God, I don't believe this. I have the wrong sets on the truck," I said. The renter responded, "What do you mean?" I said, "I apologize, but I cannot deliver these sets because they are the wrong ones. We'll have to reschedule tomorrow." The renter asked, "Can't you just give me what you have?" (Tell me that's not a red-ass flag.) "No, unfortunately I cannot do that," I replied. "The paperwork and serial numbers have to match. We'll get it straightened out tomorrow, but unfortunately I cannot leave this merchandise here in this *empty* house today." In the back of my mind, I was thinking, "I'll put you on the Do Not Rent list tomorrow too, so you don't have to worry about being in good standing again, you shady bastard!"

After that, I got the hell out of there. But would you believe after all my good work that night, my store manager was mad the next day? He told me I shouldn't make judgment calls like that, and he had me deliver the stuff to the guy anyway. I told him that delivering merchandise to that apartment was giving it away and it was a guaranteed loss. Anything delivered there would be stolen and never seen again, so I told him to give it to another account manager. He sent someone else, and you know what happened: the stuff was gone when the account manager went back to collect payment from the renter. Oh well, I'm glad I didn't take the hit.

Who to Trust When You Rent

This next story isn't about stealing or anything; it's about trust. Who should you, the renter, trust when you rent a car? The people renting you the car have no reason to lie to you, so they are probably telling you the truth when they say you are responsible for any and all damage unless you purchase the damage waiver. You just can't leave your insurance coverage situation unknown/blank, what happens if you get into an accident? That's like pissing in the wind, when you know you're going to get wet! Unfortunately, the next renter got soaking wet.

This man was some sort of contract worker. Sadly, when it came to renting a car, he was led astray by the powers that be (not the Almighty, but his employer). He was hired to work for the business for about eight months, and in his contract he cleverly negotiated a rental car. Nothing special, just a new vehicle that was good on gas for the traveling he would have to do back and forth for work purposes. He used the business's credit-card account to rent the vehicle, declining all the coverage on the contract, but the one question neither he nor the employer asked one another was "Who is actually providing insurance coverage on this vehicle while you have it?" Too bad he didn't negotiate that into his contract.

He rented the car from September 1 until his accident in late February. The accident was caused by black ice (a painful reminder of an East Coast winter). It happened on the highway when he slid on the ice, spun out, lost control, and smashed into the guardrail. He sustained only minor injuries, and thankfully so, because he was wearing his seat belt that day. The car was deemed to be totaled with the damages estimated at $11,560 plus towing and storage. As you can see, the car was demolished!

So who was going to pay for this damage? Inquiring minds want to know, right? Well, this is where it got ugly. Unfortunately for our renter, there was a loophole in the state laws that his personal insurance company could jump through in order to deny the claim legally and leave him holding the bag. And that's what happened. It seems that the insurance company only had to provide coverage for him in the rental car for the first sixty to ninety consecutive days. The company's denial was ironclad. Then there was the contract company. Since the renter was only under contract with that company and the contract did not stipulate that it would cover him as an employee driving a company-rented car—and he was not listed on the payroll as an employee— the company was not obligated to cover him either. It didn't carry insurance and had no means to give away over $11,000 anyway. So what about the credit-card coverage? We (meaning I) tried that too. But it turned out that the credit company required a call on the day he rented the car in order to activate the coverage and charge the company a premium every month on that credit card. Since that was not done, the credit-card company was a dead end too!

So congratulations on making the list, sir. I'm sorry, Mr. Renter, but you are the proud papa of an $11,000 bundle of debt, and you will never be able to rent with us again. Take care, and honestly I hope you win the lottery. That way you'll end up much better off than our next renter, Mr. Bad Choices.

The Blind-Date Debacle

This next rental story is a great example of what not to do in every way imaginable. I mean, this guy—we'll call him Ray—got it all wrong from start to finish. For starters he didn't own a vehicle and lived out of state (just right over the state line) from where he rented the car. Then he pretended the car was for business, so he used his company's credit card and business account to rent the vehicle, saying, "It's for a business dinner." All of that couldn't be further from the truth.

Ray's idea of renting a car was that you could rent for whatever reason you wanted, regardless of the truth. He had no regard for basic human decency or common sense, and I only say that because of what happened. Ray told us he was taking clients from Connecticut to Boston for a hockey game and dinner, which was why he needed the vehicle. However, we later found out that the client was one woman—a woman who didn't even know him from a hole in the ground, to put it into perspective. Basically, this was a blind date. In several phone conversations with this woman—let's call her Jen—she explained to me that he hit on her all night long because he was expecting the date to end with sex; meanwhile she had to fight him off as if she was in a sparring match. She said he was relentless and getting drunker by the minute, so she finally demanded that he take her home. The sad thing was that the ride home from Boston to the last exit in Connecticut was at least two hours, and they both had been drinking. But "it's a rental," he said. "I'm good to go. I'll stop and get a coffee." He did and they left.

They were about three-fourths of the way back to Connecticut when Ray decided he was too tired to drive anymore. He told Jen she had to drive or he'd crash, so she did. However, this was Ray's ploy to get into her house when they got there. He thought he could pretend to be incapable of driving anymore that night and she'd fall for it. So he pulled over on a dark stretch of road in the middle of nowhere, and she took the wheel. She knew her way home and was anxious to get there. Jen was probably speeding along this road when she hit a patch of black ice, and *boom*, she collided with a pole and a guardrail. The vehicle, a Dodge Ram, was demolished, but luckily they survived with minor injuries. The front end was smashed, the front wheels were completely off the vehicle, and every window was busted out. This vehicle was totaled!

In any accident, the first step of the claim process is to file a claim with the insurance company so that the insurance company can verify coverage for the driver, but keep in mind this was not just any regular old accident! The driver (Jen) and the passenger/renter (Ray) hated each other, and they both had been drinking that night. Ray had no insurance because he didn't own a car, and Jen's insurance company denied the claim because she did not rent the vehicle and had no collision coverage anyway. Still, she was responsible because she had been driving, so almost immediately Jen lawyered up. She felt that she should not be held responsible for the crash, and her lawyer called me every other day to tell me so. Ray's credit-card company even denied the claim, so he was completely on the hook for this totaled truck as well.

These are the questions I asked of myself in studying this particular claim: why would anyone lie, rent, drink and get drunk, harass and assault, and embarrass himself all in one day? Isn't that a little over the top? I think so. It was definitely enough to put the guy on the DNR list forever. Can I get an amen?

Another item on the don't-do list is dropping off a rental car somewhere other than the rental branch without notifying that branch. That's just stupid.

Don't Drop Off the Rental

Mr. Nice Guy is the man who represents an entire sect of argumentative cretins who have taken that phrase "the customer is always right" to an unprecedented level of stupidity. As I discussed in the introduction, the founders who coined the phrase did not intend for it to be abused by consumers against businesses. You have to understand something about rental-car companies: we don't want cars constantly going to the shop. It's ludicrous to think that we do. So when we discover damage on a vehicle when it's returned, don't flip out on us. Flip out *before* you drive off with your rental car and demand that the vehicle be inspected again more thoroughly if you feel it should be.

Mr. Nice Guy found himself sixty miles away from home (across state lines) at the dealership where he bought his car. The dealer would be keeping the car a few days, so he was sent over to us for a rental. After signing the contract and agreeing to the condition of the car with no damage, he left. The next day he dropped the vehicle off at the dealership without seeing or talking to anyone from the rental company. He basically gave the rental vehicle to the dealership and walked away. When we got the car and inspected it, the right front hubcap was broken with about a fourth of it missing, and the vehicle had been keyed down the entire passenger side (front bumper to rear bumper). When we called him about the damage, the plea bargaining started. "I don't know how it happened," "You can't call my insurance company," "It's not my fault," "Somebody at the dealership must have done it" … He said everything you can imagine to try to get out of this, but it didn't work. You're on the hook for this damage, sir, all $1,050 of it.

This is the best example of why you should always buy the damage waiver the rental-car company offers. A one-day rental in which the damage waiver is probably less than twenty dollars could save you hundreds, possibly thousands. Now this guy was responsible for his $500 deductible if his insurance company covered the balance. If not, his out-of-pocket expense would be more than $1,000. This was a truly sad situation. My heart goes out to this guy. Well, not really because he should have returned the car to the same people he got it from. So pay up, buddy, or you too will stay on the DNR list.

Why would you knowingly rent a car after the company inspected it but then drop it off without that same inspection process a day later? I guess that old catchphrase fits the bill here: "stupid is as stupid does." What that means is stupid people are going to keep on doing stupid things because that's what they are—just plain stupid. Just like the next renter's story, which is stupid, pathetic, and funny all at the same time.

If Men Are Dogs, How Can They Drive?

If men are dogs, what does that make women? Zoophilic? Men can be accused of many things, including adultery, but all that qualifies them for is being stupid. A cheating spouse truly is a sad thing, but ask yourself this question: if your spouse was cheating on you, how would you prefer to find out? Better yet, if you were the one cheating, how would you prefer to get caught? This is the story of Donald the renter, and I'd be willing to bet my paycheck that this is not the way he wanted to be caught.

Back in 2001, Donald rented a very nice Cadillac from us. In fact he preferred the Caddy and kept it for several weeks—until the accident, that is. Donald had an additional driver on the contract who he told us was his wife. We thought it was a little strange that they didn't have the same last name, but people do that all the time these days so we thought nothing of it. Donald and the additional driver, Jeanette, had had the vehicle for about three weeks when we got the call that they had rear-ended another car while exiting the highway. Jeanette had been driving on a suspended license. So the vehicle was towed, and the damages came out to be about $2,850. We filed a claim with Don's insurance company, and it was denied because Jeanette was not listed on the policy. So I began diligently calling and sending certified letters to Donald and Jeanette and got no response. Eventually we held both of them responsible for the damage, and we ended up sending them both to collections for nonpayment and placing them on the DNR list.

Five years later, in 2006, guess who walked into a rental branch. You guessed it, Donald and Teresa, his real wife of ten years. But when Donald's information was entered into the computer, he popped up on the DNR list with a claim number that said, "Wife Jeanette crashed vehicle, $2,850+ due in damages. Do Not Rent." This caused an instant problem. The employee, being a newbie, didn't know the history on this and simply told them what was on the screen. Teresa flipped out and said, "Who the hell is Jeanette, you lying bastard?" She let him have it, and she didn't care at all that she was in a public place. Then she turned and asked for a copy of the accident report, which we could only give to the renter. She said, "Oh, he won't mind, will you, Donald?" And he replied, "Nope, go ahead, man; give her one." So we did.

That man was cold busted. His wife was so mad; it was as if he had cheated the previous night. When she left and he started to walk behind her, she said, "Where're you going"? He said, "To the car with you." And she replied, "Oh no, I don't think so! You'd better call that cheap little hooker for a ride, because you ain't riding with me." Well, Donald, you can't stay here either, my man. You're on the DNR list so you've got to go, buddy. Good luck in divorce court!

Going the Extra Mile

If you were to ask an average renter's wife if he was a good guy or not, what kind of answer do you think you would get (barring Donald's wife of course)? Stranger things have happened in the world, but when it comes to being a good renter or even just a nice person, you will not find that person in any of the pages of this book. Especially the guy in the following story; let's call him Randy. Good ole Randy rented a pickup truck. We're not sure if he needed a truck for a specific reason, but it would have been better for us if he had rented a car because the loss wouldn't have been so high. Remember, the more valuable the vehicle, the higher the cost of repairs will be.

Although there were no issues at the outset, about a month into the rental something weird happened to Randy. While he was stopped at an intersection, he passed out cold, but the truck was still on, running and in gear. His foot slipped off the brake, and he slowly coasted into a parked car. The police were called with an ambulance, and Randy was taken to the hospital. Consequently, the police department towed our vehicle to its nearest secure tow facility. That's how it typically is supposed to happen anyway. Unfortunately, this happened on a Thursday, and we weren't notified until Friday afternoon so there wasn't enough time to get the proper documentation and the truck out of the tow yard before closing on Friday. That meant the vehicle would be sitting in the tow lot behind the barbed wire fence until Monday. That's what I told Randy when he called, after being released from the hospital, looking for the truck so he could get his stuff out of it. He didn't like it very much either, but there was nothing we could do. After I gave him that news, I heard him slam down the phone so hard he probably broke it.

Lo and behold, after our conversation was over, Randy had his own ideas about the truck. That night he jumped the fence and broke into the tow yard, smashed the glass window to get into the office, and stole the key to the truck. He found the truck, but by that time the police had responded to the alarm. Randy didn't care though; he was dead set on getting out of there one way or another. Who knew when we woke up the next morning that one of our rental vehicles would be involved in a police chase. The gates to the lot were closed, but Randy was driving a truck that could plow right through the barbed wire gates. Even the cops were shocked as he drove the truck through the fence, causing all sorts of damage. It was unbelievable to see, according to the police. They gave chase, but Randy got away and later dropped off the truck at the branch while it was closed and left the keys in the mailbox. The truck had thousands of dollars in damage. Today there's still a warrant out for his arrest, and of course he is banned from renting cars. But no one knows what he had in that truck that was worth all that trouble. It's typical that he had no insurance or credit-card coverage. This guy would appear to be one who slipped through the cracks, because we should have never rented to him in the first place. Oh well, he's on the DNR list now. I guess the one thing we can say is that at least he wasn't involved in drugs like the renter in the next story. Although, for all we know, there may have been a kilo of cocaine hidden under the seat of that truck, which would explain why he did that.

Yes, Addicts Do Make the DNR List

Addictions are a bad thing, yes, but they're even worse when they get you in trouble. That's exactly what happened to our next renter who had an odd yet popular kind of addiction (at least that's what I think). This renter probably had no idea when he woke up in the morning that his day would end as it did. All jokes aside, we were glad that he didn't die from an overdose.

One day, innocently enough, this guy parked his rental car on the street in front of a gas station for a few hours. The gas station owner found it to be a little suspicious—a guy sitting in his car fidgeting around for hours—and I can't say I blame him, so he called the police. With the way things are nowadays, he was right to call the police. After the police arrived at the gas station and the owner pointed out our rental car with the renter still sitting in it doing God knows what, the officer pulled up his cruiser right behind the rental car. No lights or sirens, just the officer parked behind the car.

After running the plate number and finding out it was a rental car, the officer approached the vehicle. As he moved closer to the driver's side door, he could see the driver sitting upright in the driver's seat with his head tilted back. When the officer reached the front door, he immediately noticed about a half dozen aerosol cans on the passenger seat. Using his baton, the officer tapped on the window to get the driver's attention, but the renter appeared to be passed out. So the officer tapped again with still no response. He walked back to his cruiser to try the loudspeaker. Upon doing so, the officer thought he saw the renter responding and moving, so he approached the driver's door again. This time, as he looked into the car, he could clearly see the driver with an aerosol can placed up to his face, spraying himself through his nose. So the officer banged on the lower part of the door as hard as he could and screamed, "Hey, you open this door and step out of the car right now!"

I'm not sure if the officer scared this guy or if it was just good timing, but according to the police report, as soon as the officer did that, the renter keeled over and went into convulsions. It was as if he was having a seizure or something, which scared the daylights out of the officer, so he did what anybody probably would have done. He smashed out the driver's door window with his baton. He reached in and unlocked the door, opened it, and pulled the renter out of the car onto the ground. By then people had started to gather around to see what the commotion was. The officer radioed for an ambulance and tried doing CPR on the renter once he stopped convulsing. He then called in the incident while people continued to gather around to watch. No one wanted to assist; they all just wanted to watch and be nosy (shameful). The officer notified dispatch about the damage to the car and asked the dispatcher to call the nearest rental branch, which is how I got all the details— that plus the actual police report. The renter made it to the hospital and was treated and released, and believe it or not, he didn't even bother to call us.

The damage to the car was a broken window and a dented door. The strange thing about this is that the damage was caused willingly and wantonly by the police officer, but there's a little secret you should know. You would think the police department would be responsible for that damage, right? Nope, not even. When the authorities are performing their job, they have what's known as "municipal immunity." The long and short of this is that they can smash your car in an emergency and not be held liable for your damages. So with this bit of good news, we headed directly to the renter for payment of the damages and guess what? He had no insurance, no job, and no money. Perfect! Just what you'd expect in a slimy situation like this one. So we just put him on the DNR list and sent him to collections. Who wants to bet on whether or not he'll try to rent from us again? They all do; it's like they purposely forget these incidents ever occurred, and there is no other rental-car company around. Crazy, right? Well, crazy is what the next renter must have eaten for breakfast because he took crazy to a new level of lunacy.

He Did the Damage and Then Some

Unlike the last guy, in this story there isn't another soul on the planet responsible for these damages—just this crazy-ass renter! This incident was not even a question of guilt or innocence either. It was actually just a question of how guilty was this guy? People do amazing things and crazy things, and this kind of falls under both categories with a big ole dose of negativity too. What you need to know is that this guy didn't have to do this; he *chose* to do it!

Let's call him David, and I'll let you know right now that he rented a new Ford pickup truck for unknown reasons. He was a young guy in 2006, twenty-two years old, and maybe that had something to do with it because men mature later in life and all that. I don't really know, but what I do know for sure is that everything he did to the vehicle was stupid, despicable, and downright crazy.

David had the truck for about a month before I got a call from the state police. They found this truck stuck at the bottom of a hill on a tree stump after it had been driven into a tree or a pole (from the obvious damage) and through the fence at the top of the hill. According to the police at the scene, it was going to take one hell of a magic trick to get this vehicle out of the abyss-like location. Oh, did I mention the power lines? Yeah, it was stuck in some power lines too. It's a bit hard to describe, but just imagine an immovable object like a crashed car stuck at the bottom of a gorge on the outskirts of town where it was lucky to be found. A tow truck wouldn't be able to drive down the hill to get the vehicle, and the vehicle wasn't drivable because the front bumper and windshield were smashed in and the undercarriage damage was extensive due to the vehicle running over the tree stump. Not to mention that power lines surrounded the truck, making it an extremely dangerous situation.

The first thing to do in a situation like this is to call the renter, and I did so after I was notified by the police department to find out what he had to say. Can you guess what David said? He swore up and down that the vehicle was stolen from him, which we later found out to be a complete lie. The police interrogated him regarding the incident, and after a few hours, he admitted to making up the car theft story to cover up the fact that he had hit a tree with the truck and didn't want to be held responsible for it. The fact of the matter was that he purposefully found this area and drove the truck off the edge of the road, through a fence, down the hill into the ditch, through some power lines, and onto the tree stump to avoid being blamed for the first accident. This guy caused an incredible amount of collision and property damage.

Needless to say, David was going on immediate DNR, but don't forget that we still needed to get our vehicle out of that ditch. It took several hours and more than one tow truck to do it too. The tow bill alone came to $1,250, and the vehicle was a total loss. Oh, and in case you were wondering, there isn't an insurance company on the planet that would pay a $1,250 tow bill and cover the total loss of a pickup truck when its insured is being investigated by the police department for causing willful and wanton property damage. Especially when he's charged and ends up pleading guilty. You've earned a life sentence on the DNR list, dude. Congratulations.

Death with No Answers

As bad as that last story seems, it isn't as bad as it can get. Because as bad as it can get usually involved some type of death in a vehicle. Sometimes we had bad situations occur with no clue of how they happened, and we were left with the cleanup after all was said and done. That's what this next situation was: a bad day for the renter and us, and a really bad day for the unauthorized driver to whom she gave the vehicle.

It was the summer of 2006, and this renter only needed the car for a few days. You see, she got the rental through a small mom-and-pop car dealership because the car she bought from the business had some minor problems. So while the dealership was fixing her car, it set her up in one of our rentals at the dealer's cost. As you may know, when a dealership or business of any kind agrees to pay for a rental car for you, that's all it's doing is paying for the rental. The business does not assume liability or responsibility of any sort for the condition of the car. In fact when you sign the contract, you are agreeing to those terms and conditions and agreeing to be responsible for anything that happens to that car no matter what. That being said, in this case it wasn't so much about any damage caused to the vehicle but more so about where the vehicle was. It turned out to be the location of the vehicle that would be the problem—that and the dead man found inside it.

A week into the rental period, we called the renter (Barbara) to see how everything was going, and to our surprise

49

she told us she didn't have the car anymore. According to Barbara, she returned the car to the folks at the dealership three days ago and had her new car back. When we asked her why she didn't call us to advise us that she was returning the rental vehicle, she said that the dealership people told her they would take care of it and she didn't have to bother with any of that, so she didn't. This all sounded very fishy, but to be honest with you, it wasn't unusual; this type of thing happened at dealerships and body shops all the time. They would tell their customers to bring our car to them when the rental period was over instead of returning it to us. They thought they were offering great customer service. But, hey, who am I to tell you that you signed a legally binding contract and you probably shouldn't listen to the moron who tells you to do something that sounds fairly stupid.

This time, however, it was a little more fishy than usual because apparently the salesman wanted to keep the rental car for himself for a while, several weeks to be exact. That means we had a stolen vehicle on our hands. After we called the renter, we called the dealership immediately to speak with her salesman, Matt, since he was the one who spearheaded this whole thing. All we got from the dealership for two weeks was "He's not here, and the car is not here." It turned out to be true too. He was not there or at home; in fact his wife also was looking for him. Then out of the blue I got a call from the New Hampshire State Police. It seems they found our vehicle out there in a vacant lot; only the vehicle was not empty. A man was in the car, and he was dead. There was no obvious cause of death that the police could tell me over the phone. No blood in the car, no damage to the car either, just a dead man who unfortunately turned out to be Matt, the car salesman.

Although this case didn't fit into our typical set of claims, it still resulted in the renter going on the DNR list. Although the unfortunate death of the salesman was the peak part of this story, the main thing to remember is that he was an unauthorized driver, and the car was stolen during that whole three-week period. Contract violations and a stolen vehicle are enough to make the DNR list, let alone a death resulting from those violations. In no way did it mean that the blame for the death of the salesman was someone's fault, particularly the renter. The police didn't even have any explanations for the cause of death, and we had no idea why he took the car to New Hampshire. It was just an unfortunate part of some very bad circumstances, and may God rest his soul. This was an unsolved mystery that remains unsolved today.

A Bad Move by This Renter

In the car rental business, you don't necessarily come across bad things every day. It's just that when these bad things do happen, they are unforgettable. Like our next renter/genius who left us a little surprise in the car—an unwanted surprise.

If you've ever rented a car, you know that there's an inspection of the car when you pick it up and bring it back. While no two individuals will ever inspect a car exactly the same way, it should be pointed out that the inspections are done. So when Jeff rented a car, we had to drive the car up to the inspection point (directly in front of the glass windows of the office), leave the key in the ignition, get out, and inspect the entire vehicle with Jeff and whomever is looking out of the window (normally other employees). So there was no question that the inspection was done as usual. Jeff was a very tall man, the kind of tall man who would have to push the driver's seat back as far as it would go to be even remotely comfortable while driving the vehicle. I know because this is what I have to do at six foot three, and our resident genius, Jeff, was at least six foot five, probably six foot six. I point this out because it is the key ingredient in the circumstances that unfolded.

I guess Jeff only needed the car for a week because that's when he dropped it off at our branch while we were closed (a week later). When we checked the car to close out his contract, we got our surprise. Jeff had left the driver's seat all the way back, so when our car prep guy got into the vehicle, he (being only five foot five) fell back into the seat. Naturally he moved the seat up, and that's when he heard a clanking sound as if something was stuck under the seat. He moved the seat all the way back and quickly jammed it forward and *bam*! There at his feet was a black 9mm semiautomatic Glock handgun that had popped out from under the seat. Wow! Who the hell leaves (what we later found out to be) a *loaded* semiautomatic handgun in a car that does not belong to you?

There was definitely something wrong with this picture. Should our first call have been to the renter to come and pick up his loaded weapon or to the local police department to report the found loaded weapon? What would you do? Don't worry, I did the right thing and called the police, but let me tell you why. Once the car prep found the gun, I made sure no one touched it. You have no way of knowing when or where that handgun was last seen or used, and the minute you put your fingerprints on that handgun without knowing that information, that last crime now belongs to you. And if your prints are in the system, you're definitely screwed because they'll find you ten times faster even though you didn't do anything. So I told my rental team that we'd call the police and put Mr. Not So Bright on the DNR list for leaving a loaded weapon in the car. If he came to the branch looking for lost-and-found, we'd just tell him that the item he was looking for was at One Police Plaza, and he had a reservation there waiting for him to pick up his loaded semiautomatic weapon. That was back in 2001, and ten years later, in 2011, he was still on the DNR list. When you do something that stupid, you can make a name for yourself on the DNR list quickly and easily, without owing money or damaging any cars. A nice simple story like the next one.

The Repo Man

This is not a story of making the DNR list per se; it's more like a state of affairs and how bad things can get for some people. When I rented furniture and appliances to people, it got really bad every week. Basically, the way the system worked was that when customers came in and rented merchandise, they would become my new account. They rented weekly, which means their payment had to be in our office every Monday morning. Most people would use the drop box over the weekend to pay, and if they didn't, they would come into the office to pay on Monday or Tuesday.

By the end of the day on Monday, we had a list of everyone who paid—and everyone who didn't. On Tuesday we would start calling accounts to remind those whose payment was overdue, leaving messages and paging them (this was back in 1997) so they could call us back to discuss their situation.

Their signed rental agreement with us stated that if at any time they did not have the money to pay for the merchandise, they would return the merchandise willingly. They could always get the stuff back as long as they returned it willingly; we would hold on to it until they had the money. This is how the contract was written. So on Tuesdays we spent all day making phone calls, and if we had no contact with renters, then we spent every Wednesday, Thursday, Friday, and Saturday going to their houses and picking up the merchandise or collecting the money. Believe me when I tell you that you've never seen such a sad look on someone's face as when you go to his or her house to take the living room set, the bed, the TV, or the washer and dryer.

One time I had to repo the furniture from a customer, and that furniture happened to be her kids' bunk beds. It was probably the single most awful thing I encountered on that job, and it probably messed up those kids for life too. Here's how it played out: I went to the house, knocked on the door, and one of the kids answered. I said, "Hi, is your mom home?" The kid said yes and went to get her. Well, this was a Friday, do-or-die day in this business because your next payment is due on Sunday, so she'd know what I was there for. Sure enough, as soon as she walked up to me and saw the company van in front of the house, she said, "Come on in and take it." That's all she wrote!

I spent the next two hours disassembling a very nice wooden bunk bed set while four little kids literally sat adjacent to me, watching me unscrew every bolt and stack every wooden plank. It was the equivalent of taking away their Christmas presents. That was a sad, awful day for those kids and me. Even now I wish I could go back and change that day.

Are You Serious?

Without a doubt this next story involves one of the top three worst renters we'd ever had. I mean, there are some things that you just don't do, and he did each and every one of those things anyway. In the end he lost, because now he's on the DNR list for life. I just hope that no one accidentally takes him off DNR, allowing him to rent once again.

It started with renting him (John) a car back in 2004. When he received the rental car, unfortunately there was no way to tell what kind of person he was or what his intentions were. You just had to go with the flow and hope it turned out for the best when you rented someone a car. After renting the car for about the first three days, he abruptly stopped paying for it as if he just didn't have to "rent" the rental car anymore. None of us knew what this guy's deal was or what to expect, but days went by and days turned into weeks with no contact and no payment from the renter. At a certain point we contacted the police department and reported the car stolen. A vehicle stolen from us by the renter meant the police would have all of his personal information in full detail. However, even with that, weeks still went by, and we'd lost this car to John.

Then five weeks later, a shimmer of hope came when the police called to say they'd located the car. The shimmer of hope quickly turned into dismay. They found the car all right, because it was involved in an accident and totaled. You would think that would be the end of the story but not quite. After stealing the car from us, totaling it in an accident, and never bothering to call us, John had the nerve to walk into the branch looking for a replacement car. *Are you serious?* That was the question of the day when he walked into the branch; it was absolutely unbelievable. After being told "no" several times by several people, including the branch manager and his boss, John continued to demand another car. It got tense when he started to threaten the employees and really show his ass (so to speak) as if he deserved customer service. Finally the police were called, and he was escorted out with the threat of handcuffs. The capper to this situation was that he had no insurance, no money, and no intention of being an upstanding, responsible person and paying for the damages, but we should have given him another car? *Are you serious?*

John went on the DNR list as soon as he stole the car from us and didn't bother to return our calls or respond to our letters. It wasn't a matter of something personal against him or anything like that; we wanted nothing more than to get paid for our damages and losses. Thus, the next thing we did was file litigation against John so we could sue him and get a judgment against him for our damages, which we did and we won. He even showed up in court and tried to deny things, but the judge wasn't buying it. We were there personally, and it was quite laughable to see him try to blow smoke up the judge's ass as he did to us when he stole the car. He was guilty, and we won our case against him, getting a judgment for him to pay us the $10,500 in damages that he owed. God knows he wasn't going to pay us one red cent, but in case he hit the lottery or something, we at least had a judgment against him so we could be the first ones in line to get paid from his riches. Now that should be the end of the story, but it's not!

Believe it or not, two years later this man walked into the same branch to rent a car *again*! Fortunately for him there was an entirely new staff in the branch, so no one recognized him. However, when he popped up on the DNR list and they read how much trouble he'd caused and how much money he owed, the staff denied him a rental. This guy had the nerve to try denying everything, and get this: he said, "It wasn't me; it must have been identity theft." That was classic, and he stuck to the story wholeheartedly. He said he refused to leave without a car, so the staff called me over to the branch to try and talk this guy down and out of the building. Now I'm no slouch, and I was the expert on company policy and the laws governing this ordeal, so I did my best to gently talk this guy into leaving. But after the third time he said "It wasn't me; it was identity theft," I'd had enough. This guy had to go!

I told him straight out, "Look, you're not getting a car today or any other day from this branch or any of our other branches, so give it up. Leave now without police assistance and you can at least still have your dignity, or you can wait and leave in handcuffs. I personally saw you in court for this prior claim, and no one wants to steal your identity. Your identity sucks." He responded with several expletives, so I had to walk him to the door. He was a tough nut to crack, but finally getting him out the door was a pleasure, except for the middle finger and the other expletives he threw at me outside. It just goes to show that truly the customer is *not* always right. As our next lovely patron was quoted as saying, "I just tapped a pole." I didn't know a pole could do that kind of damage to a car.

<u>I Just Tapped a Pole</u>

In the true definition of what can only be described as a "bad renter," this next case takes the cake when it comes to stupid explanations, dumb comebacks, and a special kind of ignorance. It was a shame that we rented him a new Cadillac. I believe the renter was drunk when he called the rental branch to say that the car was damaged and needed to be towed away. I say that because his exact words to the branch were "I just tapped a pole and messed up the fender."

We never knew whether the "pole" was left standing or not, but from the condition of the vehicle (as you can see), parts of his story were missing. So we immediately put this man on the DNR list both to prevent further losses on any other vehicles and to pressure him into telling us the truth about what happened to this vehicle. Nevertheless, he held out on the truth during the entire claims process, and when he found that we had put him on the DNR list, he flipped out and demanded to speak with the top man in charge of rentals. When he got to the top man, he got his way and was taken off DNR, because according to this man, he was a preferred customer. He believed he was entitled to get a Cadillac every time he rented.

That first Cadillac he rented and basically totaled was covered by his insurance company, but the process we (meaning me) had to go through to achieve the end result was incredible. Why? Because this guy was very clever. First of all, he never gave us his insurance information when he rented, and secondly, he disagreed with the amount of the damage estimated for the Cadillac. He refused to willingly give us his insurance information when our claim was initiated. I had to look up his previous rentals until we found one in which he rented under an insurance claim. Then I called the adjuster from the other insurance company (which was paying for his rental car) and asked her the name and policy/claim number she had on file for this man. I was able to get the information from her and then get a claim filed under his policy. Of course he was upset and belligerent because I was able to do this, but the fact of the matter was that we lost a luxury vehicle due to his negligence, and that was unacceptable. However, his conversation (likely filled with threats) with the man in charge earned him the privilege of renting with us once again.

Lo and behold, this man's next rental of a Cadillac months later ended the same way with the car damaged and not drivable. That was convincing enough for the man in charge to place this negligent renter back on the DNR list *permanently*. Of course this accident was not the renter's fault either, according to him. This time he was quoted as saying, "I just got a flat tire, but the car can't drive." That flat tire turned out to be a broken axle shaft and smashed wheel assembly. That costs a little bit more than a flat tire, buddy. Sometimes a flat tire can be fixed for free.

The End

DNR is the customers getting what they deserve or reaping what they've sown—
because
the customer is not always right!

The Do Not Rent List II

has a
$500 prize
waiting for you if you have
the best DNR story.

Write to me with your Do Not Rent story so it can be published in the next book. I want to produce the best Do Not Rent story of all time. So I am challenging you all to email me with your story or one you know of so it can win the title: "Do Not Rent" Story of the Year. Please e-mail your stories to me at TheDoNotRentListII.vpweb.com to enter the contest. Your entry will be heavily scrutinized, and you may be contacted to confirm its validity. Your story must be true and supported by some sort of documentation, such as a police report, an incident or accident report, or some other written documentation that will validate your story. Again, all stories will be subject to a rigorous level of scrutiny and must be verified before they can be published. Welcome to:

The "Do Not Rent" List II.

About the Author

Todd Ruffin is a father, an author, a veteran soldier and a businessman, in that order. He amassed well over 25 years of business experience working at the management level of some of the nations top customer service oriented businesses. He received his Master's Degree from one the most highly recognized hospitality/business colleges in the nation, Johnson & Wales University. He used that education, his expertise and his own personal experiences on the job to write this book. The situations were real and unforgiving.

If after you read this book Todd Ruffin hasn't made you think so deeply about the reality of customer service in the United States so that the next time you are in a store or anywhere buying something you don't look around you and survey the patrons nearest you for trouble. Well then his job was not done!

Printed in the United States
By Bookmasters